TONY BENNETT

S T E P P I N ' O U T

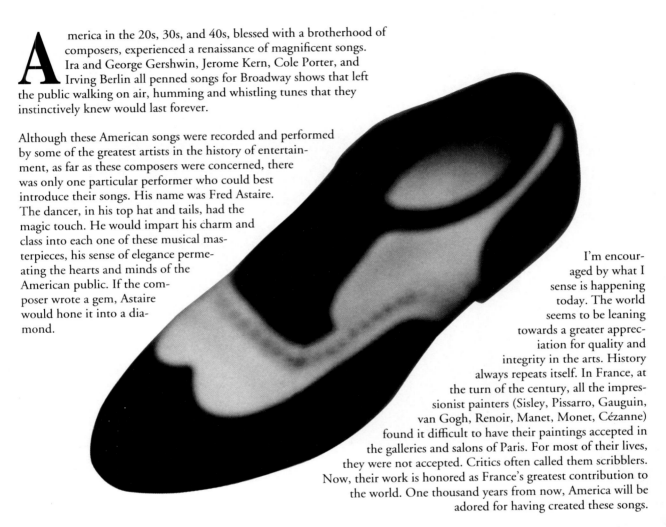

America in the 20s, 30s, and 40s, blessed with a brotherhood of composers, experienced a renaissance of magnificent songs. Ira and George Gershwin, Jerome Kern, Cole Porter, and Irving Berlin all penned songs for Broadway shows that left the public walking on air, humming and whistling tunes that they instinctively knew would last forever.

Although these American songs were recorded and performed by some of the greatest artists in the history of entertainment, as far as these composers were concerned, there was only one particular performer who could best introduce their songs. His name was Fred Astaire. The dancer, in his top hat and tails, had the magic touch. He would impart his charm and class into each one of these musical masterpieces, his sense of elegance permeating the hearts and minds of the American public. If the composer wrote a gem, Astaire would hone it into a diamond.

I'm encouraged by what I sense is happening today. The world seems to be leaning towards a greater appreciation for quality and integrity in the arts. History always repeats itself. In France, at the turn of the century, all the impressionist painters (Sisley, Pissarro, Gauguin, van Gogh, Renoir, Manet, Monet, Cézanne) found it difficult to have their paintings accepted in the galleries and salons of Paris. For most of their lives, they were not accepted. Critics often called them scribblers. Now, their work is honored as France's greatest contribution to the world. One thousand years from now, America will be adored for having created these songs.

As a tunesmith, I'm convinced, that these American masterpieces will be our finest cultural contribution to the world, and Fred Astaire our national treasure.

—Tony Bennett

Management: Danny Bennett
RPM Music Productions, Inc.
101 West 55 Street
New York, NY 10019

Album Art Direction: Arnold Levine/Allen Weinberg
Photography: Lois Greenfield

Special thanks to Frank Military for collecting all the songs for the album

CONTENTS

STEPPIN' OUT WITH MY BABY

Words and Music by
IRVING BERLIN

WHO CARES?
(So Long As You Care For Me)

Music and Lyrics by
GEORGE GERSHWIN
and IRA GERSHWIN

TOP HAT, WHITE TIE AND TAILS

Words and Music by
IRVING BERLIN

THEY CAN'T TAKE THAT AWAY FROM ME

Music and Lyrics by
GEORGE GERSHWIN
and IRA GERSHWIN

mel- o- dy ling-ers on. They may take you from me, I'll miss your fond ca-

ress. But though they take you from me, I'll still pos - sess:

Refrain (not fast)
The way you wear your hat, ___ The way you sip your tea, ___

slowly with warmth

The mem'ry of all that _____ No, no! They can't take that a-way from me!

DANCING IN THE DARK

Words by
HOWARD DIETZ

Music by
ARTHUR SCHWARTZ

A SHINE ON YOUR SHOES

Words by
HOWARD DIETZ

Music by
ARTHUR SCHWARTZ

Don't you be a good for noth-in', Nev-er 'mount to noth-in', Hang-in' round the cor-ners!

Can't you see you nev-er will be get-tin' an-y-where.

You'll find a lot in what I'm re- peat - ing___ "When there's a
shine on your shoes, There's a mel-o-dy in your heart;" What a
won- der- ful way to start the day. When there's a
day.___ (to Patter) day.___

HE LOVES AND SHE LOVES

Music and Lyrics by
GEORGE GERSHWIN
and IRA GERSHWIN

THEY ALL LAUGHED

Music and Lyrics by
GEORGE GERSHWIN
and IRA GERSHWIN

I CONCENTRATE ON YOU

Words and Music by
COLE PORTER

YOU'RE ALL THE WORLD TO ME

By
BURTON LANE
and ALAN JAY LERNER

Lively Fox Trot

You're like Paris in A-pril and May___
You're Lake Co-mo when dawn is a-glow___

You're New York on a sil-ver-y day___
You're Sun Val-ley right af-ter a snow___

A Swiss Alp as the sun grows faint-er; You're Loch
A mu-se-um, a Per-sian pa-lace, You're my

Lo-mond when Au-tumn is the paint-er You're moon-light on a
shin-ing Au-ro-ra Bo-re-a-lis You're like Christ-mas at

ALL OF YOU

Words and Music by
COLE PORTER

NICE WORK IF YOU CAN GET IT

Music and Lyrics by
GEORGE GERSHWIN
and IRA GERSHWIN

IT ONLY HAPPENS WHEN I DANCE WITH YOU

Words and Music by
IRVING BERLIN

SHALL WE DANCE?

Music and Lyrics by
GEORGE GERSHWIN
and IRA GERSHWIN

YOU'RE EASY TO DANCE WITH

Words and Music by
IRVING BERLIN

CHANGE PARTNERS

Words and Music by
IRVING BERLIN

danced with him since the mu-sic be - gan,_____ Won't you

CHANGE PART-NERS and dance with me?_____

Must you dance_____ quite so close_____

With your lips_____ touch-ing his face?_____ Can't you

(Melody)

CHEEK TO CHEEK

Words and Music by
IRVING BERLIN

Heav-en, _____ I'm in Heav-en. _____

And my heart beats so that I can hard-ly speak.

I GUESS I'LL HAVE TO CHANGE MY PLAN

Words by
HOWARD DIETZ

Music by
ARTHUR SCHWARTZ

THAT'S ENTERTAINMENT

Words by
HOWARD DIETZ

Music by
ARTHUR SCHWARTZ

BY MYSELF

Words by
HOWARD DIETZ

Music by
ARTHUR SCHWARTZ

Moderately

slowly

The

par-ty's o-ver, the game is end-ed, the dreams I dreamed went up in smoke. They did-n't pan out as in-tend-ed.